Opening a Cupcake Shop

How to Start a Cupcake Business from Scratch

by Marcella Mickels

Table of Contents

Introduction 1

Chapter 1: Creating a Solid Business Plan 7

Chapter 2: Naming Your Business 11

Chapter 3: Selecting a Retail Store Location 17

Chapter 4: Getting a Permit to Operate 23

Chapter 5: Acquiring Equipment and Manpower 27

Chapter 6: Marketing and Advertising 35

Conclusion 41

Introduction

The cupcake business is one of the most fun and rewarding businesses today. It's also very profitable since everybody loves cupcakes – kids, teens, and adults alike adore this delicious mini cake and its sugary frosting. Cupcakes are always in-demand for all kinds of occasions, whether it's a child's birthday, a baptism party, a wedding reception, a graduation party, a business meeting, or even a product launching. Cupcakes are always on the scene and people will always enjoy them because, not only are they tasty, but they bring a sense of 'home' and 'delight' to the table.

Starting a cupcake business can be a lucrative venture because the overhead is low, profit margins can be high, and the work is generally fun. Typically, people who start a cupcake business have a love for baking, thus going into a cupcake business is the obvious, enjoyable choice. Anybody who has baking skills can start a cupcake business because they already know their product. However, there are still plenty of other things you'll need to understand before opening a cupcake shop. Selling a few baked goods out of your home is very different from operating a cupcake shop.

This book will help you learn everything that you need to know in running a cupcake business from *outside* your home. If you are an aspiring cupcake shop owner, this book will teach you the ins and outs of the process. On top of the basics, you will also find useful tips on how to keep your business operating smoothly once it's off the ground and running. I hope this book serves you as a guide through your journey to cupcake success!

© Copyright 2014 by LCPublifish LLC - All rights reserved.

This document is geared towards providing reliable information in regard to the topic and issue covered. The publication is sold with the idea that the publisher is not required to render accounting, officially permitted, or otherwise, qualified services. If advice is necessary, legal or professional, a practiced individual in the profession should be ordered.

- From a Declaration of Principles which was accepted and approved equally by a Committee of the American Bar Association and a Committee of Publishers and Associations.

In no way is it legal to reproduce, duplicate, or transmit any part of this document in either electronic means or in printed format. Recording of this publication is strictly prohibited and any storage of this document is not allowed unless with written permission from the publisher. All rights reserved.

The information provided herein is stated to be truthful and consistent, in that any liability, in terms of inattention or otherwise, by any usage or abuse of any policies, processes, or directions contained within is solely and completely the responsibility of the recipient reader. Under no circumstances will any legal responsibility or blame be held against the publisher for any reparation, damages, or monetary loss due to the information herein, either directly or indirectly.

Respective authors own all copyrights not held by the publisher.

The information herein is offered for informational purposes solely, and is universal as so. The presentation of the information is without contract or any type of guarantee assurance.

The trademarks that are used are without any consent, and the publication of the trademark is without permission or backing by the trademark owner. All trademarks and brands within this book are for clarifying purposes only and are the owned by the owners themselves, not affiliated with this document.

Chapter 1: Creating a Solid Business Plan

All businesses should start with the creation of a sound business plan. But why is the business plan so essential? Creating a plan helps an entrepreneur identify important details such as the startup costs, operation expenses, management, equipment needs, manpower and staffing requirements, plans for marketing and advertising, and so forth. Without a thoroughly written plan for the business, small yet important details can be overlooked. So, if you want every critical detail covered, then create a plan for your cupcake business.

A business plan will help you determine how many people you need to hire, how much money you need to run the shop, and how many cupcakes you need to sell every day, every month and every year in order to break even, or better yet, turn a profit. The business plan will keep you, as an entrepreneur, focused on the things that need to be done in order to run the business successfully.

These days, having a business plan is a must. It's the first step you take to ensure the success of your business. It's equally necessary for you as a small business, as it would be for any larger business or corporation. The most important reason to have this plan is so that you have a written guide and practical plan to follow as you operate your business. Even home-based businesses are encouraged to prepare a written plan. Also, if you're going to be applying for a loan, then keep in mind banks and other investors will more likely accept highly detailed and well-prepared business plans in exchange for funding. Therefore, you'll be using this plan not only to outline your operations, but also to obtain the financial backing that you need to start and operate everything. A good plan reflects that an entrepreneur exudes professionalism, and is serious about running a successful business – both of which are attractive to investors and financial institutions when it comes to shelling out money.

If you don't have experience creating a business plan, there's a great (and inexpensive) book written by Ryan Dukes called "How to Write a Business Plan: A Step by Step Guide" that will walk you through the steps of writing your own business plan in a really simple and straightforward way. (www.amazon.com/dp/B00OTVH3GA/). In any case, never dismiss the business plan and its importance. Keep in mind that it's the first step in starting a successful business; therefore, you can't just skip it. Invest your time in creating a solid plan and you'll be on the road to success!

Chapter 2: Naming Your Business

Choosing the name for your cupcake shop is as important as choosing a name for your child. Maybe even more important actually, since the name will become the brand used to appeal to your customer base. It should not be taken for granted and careful thought and consideration must be given. Countless businesses have failed partly due to names that were poorly chosen. The name you choose for your cupcake business will be your products' brand name. You might want to select a name other than the name of your favorite person, color, celebrity, and so on. Remember, this is the name that will be associated with your products and the name will be what you promote and advertise. The name is one of the first things your potential customers will notice, so give it some serious thought before making a final decision. So, how can you choose a good brand name?

It should mean something to you.

Your business name should have meaning to you. That way, you have a personal connection with it. Just imagine that, years from now, when your business is a great success, people will be asking how you came up with the shop's name. If you name your business something that is meaningful to you such as your name or your child's name, then it will provide inspiration as you go through your business journey.

Be inspired by others.

If you need help with names and if you don't want to use your own name, parent's name, kid's name, or spouses' name, then you can always look up other cupcake shops. You can get an idea about what others in your field have chosen. Get inspiration from these, but be careful not to copy any of them. You might have trouble with your brand's identity if your name is too similar to another. You might also encounter problems with registering your business.

People should be able to remember it.

The name of your cupcake business will help you promote your brand and establish the product, so be sure to choose well. Choose something that people can easily remember. Avoid foreign words that most customers can't pronounce and keep the spelling simple. Don't choose names with complicated spelling, silent letter sounds, or too many letters and words. Just keep it simple for your customers. After all, you won't want them to have a hard time writing it or pronouncing it when they recommend it to their friends. For example, don't call it "Lisa's Kupcake

Shop" because you're always going to have to give a long explanation when you tell people "Cupcake is spelled with a 'K' as the first letter instead of a 'C'". Maybe the idea of it doesn't bother you now, but it will eventually – around the 100th time you're giving the spelling spiel. Not to mention you may lose out on customers who have heard how great your cupcakes are, but can't find your business because of the misspelling.

Search the state's business registry and consider website domains.

You may want to search the list of businesses that are registered within your state already, to make sure that you don't choose a name you'll be unable to register. Most states have a place within their secretary of state's website where you can search for any existing variations of a name you're potentially interested in. Try googling "search business names <insert your state name>". That should get you to the right website.

The same goes for website domains. If you plan on marketing over the internet, you may want to have a website, right? Ideally, you'll want it to be www.< the name of your business >.com, so you may want to see if the domain is already taken. If it is, go for a variation, or pick a different name altogether.

Consider the future of your business.

Before you finalize the business name, consider how your shop might expand or change well into the future. Rebranding your business later will be much more difficult, so before you decide on "Cupcakes Anonymous" or "We Are Cupcakes" or "Lizzy-lu's Cupcake Shop" …… think it through. Might you eventually decide to branch out and offer other baked goods, like cookies, croissants, or wedding cakes? What if those other baked goods do really well, and you're no longer just a cupcake shop? If this happens, will you wish you had gone with "Cupcakes and More" or "Lizzy-lu's Bakery Shop"? I'm not saying that's a certainty, and that you should widen your net unnecessarily. It's just something you should at least consider and then make a thoughtful decision about. There is something to be said for being specific, so if you think cupcakes is the way of your future, then it may be best to keep the word "cupcake" in your shop's name.

Test a few names first.

Why not work your way to three different options, and then test them around town amongst friends, family, and perhaps even strangers with a quick "Hey, which name is better?" survey? Since all the names have been stirring around your head for a while, it's good to get a few fresh opinions. And who knows, maybe the people you ask will have another idea for you that you end up liking even better!

Go with your gut.

Ultimately, just go with your gut. You're the one that will be promoting the business, looking at and speaking the same name multiple times daily, so you might as well end up with something you're most excited about. As long as you have passion and enthusiasm about it, others will catch on too.

Don't rush when it comes to selecting a good name for your cupcake business. Take as much time as you need and when you have something in mind, try writing it on a piece of paper so you can see how it looks written down. Some entrepreneurs overlook the double entendre of their business names and it winds up being too late to change the name later on when the business is registered and in full operation. You can also ask a second opinion if you have a questionable choice. The choosing of a business name or product name is critical as this can affect the success of the business.

Chapter 3: Selecting a Retail Store Location

Location is everything when it comes to the 'brick-and-mortar' retail world. The location of your cupcake shop can have a great effect on sales and eventually, on the success of your business. You need to put location at the top of your list of priorities. Keep in mind that you'll have higher sales if your store is located at a spot where your target customers will pass by. This is why choosing your location is one of the most important decisions that you need to make in opening your shop. There are some things you need to consider in selecting a good spot for your shop.

Consider Your Demographics

Who are your target customers? If they are students, then be sure to locate your store near a school. If your customers are the general public, then choose a location where many people have access. You can also conduct a study or a survey to help you determine spots where your target customers tend to be, or you can conduct a survey at a location you're considering to find out if nearby residents and workers might become customers.

Accessible Location

The more accessible your cupcake shop, the higher your sales will be. It's simple logic. More people can get to your product easily if your store is on the first floor of a commercial building and near the street. Is there lots of foot traffic? Or is there nearby convenient parking? Do people need to park miles away and walk to your store just to buy your cupcakes? Do they need to go up a few floors in a building? That can turn off potential customers. So, keep in mind that it's easier for customers to buy your product if your store has easy access.

Neighborhood

When choosing a location for your shop, you need to look into the neighborhood demographics and statistics. What kind of shops are in that block? Is the neighborhood safe? These are the things that you need to consider. So even if the rent is cheap in a particular block and the store size is perfect, if the shops around you are questionable and the neighborhood is unsafe, you probably want to find another location.

Staying Near the Competition

Your competition, especially if it's a big store, may have spent a large amount of money in determining the best location for their store. When you choose a store near your competition, you can reap the benefits of their marketing efforts. Your competitor's customers will also see you and will have the option to buy from them or you. Besides, you can watch your competition closely and learn their tricks – using them to improve your products and marketing.

Negotiating the Lease

After choosing a good location for your store, the work isn't finished. You still need to talk to the owner of the building about a lease. This part is as important as choosing the location because you will need to cut a deal that works for you and your business. Use your business plan as the basis for your budget, or vice versa, make sure that the cost of the lease fits within your business plan. Also, ask your lawyer to review the lease contract before you sign. They can explain the details that you might not fully understand. Don't sign anything or agree to anything yet before you've understand all the stipulations in the contract.

Asking Help from a Real Estate Professional

Real estate people know their field backward and forward. They also have an idea about the kind of people that live in each neighborhood. You could consult with a real estate professional if you think they can help you find the best location for your shop.

After choosing the best spot for your store, it pays to learn more about the location. Doing this can help you face any problems later on that involve the location of your shop. Also, it will help you determine what kind of cupcakes to make! For example, if you're near a university whose mascot is a Bumble Bee, then you're probably going to want to have a few Bumble Bee themed cupcakes in the display window.

Chapter 4: Getting a Permit to Operate

All new businesses need to get registered and obtain a license. However, for a cupcake business, there are more requirements, and one of these is the need to meet the requirements set by the local health department as well as the state health department. The requirements for home-based cupcake businesses are different from those that operate in a commercial location.

You need to be aware of the business-related laws and the licensing requirements in your state. Then, apply for the proper permit and pass the sanitation inspection before the official opening.

Business License

Obtaining a business permit or license is yet another necessary task. First, you'll need to visit the local county clerk office or the state's office (or website) to get information. While there, you'll discover the requirements for registering your business. Just fill out the necessary forms and complete all requirements for obtaining a business license. You'll need to decide whether to operate as a Sole Proprietorship, a

Partnership, a LLC, or a Corporation. Typically, if you're starting the company by yourself, a Sole Proprietorship will be less expensive, although a LLC will offer better protection from various risks. I'm not qualified to advise you on this matter, so my best advice would be to speak to a business formation attorney about it, or at least do a lot of research online to determine which type of entity works best for you. Also, the different business types have different tax implications, so it's also a good idea to speak with an accountant before choosing, or again – at least do a lot of research online in terms of the tax advantages and disadvantages of each structure.

Federal Tax ID Number

For sole business owners, it's not necessary to obtain an Employer Identification Number. Instead, they can just use their Social Security Number for the income taxes. However, partnerships, LLCs, and corporations need to obtain an IRS Tax ID number. It's very easy to do actually, by going to the irs.gov website and applying for an Employer Identification Number (EIN) online. If you do it online, you can get one instantly.

Food-Service Approval

A health inspection by the local and state health department is necessary to make sure that the food you will be selling doesn't endanger the public. The cupcake shop must pass this sanitation inspection before selling any food items. When the shop passes inspection, the food-service approval is given and you can open for business. In case your store doesn't pass the health inspection, you will be given pointers on how to improve and make it pass the next time around. The health department will give you a set period of time and several more chances to meet the health and sanitation requirements.

Once you obtain a business license and have gone through the health inspection process, you are on your way to becoming a successful cupcake entrepreneur. You have achieved one of the most important steps in starting a cupcake shop business!

Chapter 5: Acquiring Equipment and Manpower

Before you can open your cupcake business, there are still things you need to complete. One is the equipment needed to run a cupcake business. Investing in high quality equipment is crucial since these are your main tools in creating your product. Once you have obtained the bakery equipment, then you are one-step closer to finally opening your business and making sales.

Hiring staff is also necessary in running a cupcake business. You'll need additional manpower since you can't do all the work by yourself. Here are some tips for obtaining equipment and hiring employees.

Equipment

Before you can run a cupcake business, you need to have the basic equipment. Bakery equipment such as an oven, commercial mixers, molds, baking pans, and measuring utensils are all necessary to start a cupcake shop. There are other minor tools needed as well, such as a mixing bowl, decorating tools, spatulas, cupcake stands and wrappers. In your store, you'll need display cases, carryout boxes, containers, and much more. Be sure to purchase all the necessary equipment to make and sell cupcakes.

When it comes to kitchen appliances and bakery equipment, it is recommended that you invest in the best tools possible. There are many brands of ovens and mixers, but the most expensive ones are usually the most durable, safest, and most effective. So, if you are planning to run a cupcake business, buy the best oven and mixer that you can get. Consider these as great initial investments. Cheap bakery equipment will often break down which could cause accidents as well as production issues. Buying a high-quality oven and commercial mixer will pay off since they'll work for longer and produce better products than the cheaper kind.

If you invest in good ovens and mixers, then you can skimp on the minor tools such as measuring cups and spatulas. Unlike the oven and the mixer, these tools can be used for some time and are easily replaced. Here is a list of necessary cupcake-making equipment as a starting point:

1. Kitchen timer
2. Cake tester
3. Spatulas
4. Wooden spoons
5. Bowls in assorted sizes
6. Flour sieve or sifter
7. Kitchen scales
8. Food processor
9. Frosting knife
10. Piping bags and nozzles
11. Measuring spoons
12. Measuring cups
13. Cupcake liners
14. Cupcake trays in standard and assorted shapes
15. Cupcake stands
16. Cooling racks

Hiring Staff

Running your own cupcake shop can be fun. Finally, you are your own boss and you have control over every part of your business' operation. However, what happens when you get an order for a hundred cupcakes for tomorrow? As a good entrepreneur, you need to know when it's time to hire people to help.

The Kitchen Staff

When you first started planning your business, you may have envisioned yourself doing all the measuring, mixing, baking, icing decorating, and also doing cashier work and serving your customers. In reality, you can't do all of these tasks. Therefore, you need to hire employees to help you get things done. Since cupcakes are your main product, of course you'll need to hire people who know how to make cupcakes. Even if you're skilled, you need someone to help or fill-in for you in case you're occupied with something else. Depending on how good the business is, you need to decide whether or not to increase your kitchen staff. You can get a person to do all the measuring, one to do all the baking, one to so all the decorating, and one to wash and clean all the tools and equipment.

Counter Staff

If you will be baking or overlooking the whole kitchen operation, you'll need a person to take the telephone and in-person orders, serve the customers, and handle the cash register. And if you decide to have a dining area, you'll need even more employees. Of course, you will need to figure out exactly how many people for counter work and base it on the number of customers you usually have during peak hours.

Delivery, Cleaning, and Maintenance

Even after passing the health and sanitation inspection, your duty to provide clean surroundings for your business and customers continues. Local as well as state health departments often do drop-in inspections on restaurants and food businesses to make sure they're still complying with the health and sanitation requirements. It's important that cleanliness is maintained in your store in order to avoid any health problems and complaints from your customers.

In your business plan, you should include details on the equipment as well as the number of employees you need in order to run your cupcake business smoothly. Factor all of these numbers into the total cost and budget, and compare them against the expected sales and income to make sure you're still in the profit-making zone. □

Chapter 6: Marketing and Advertising

You might already be aware that there are numerous cupcake businesses in your area. Don't let that discourage you though. Cupcakes are very popular and are always in-demand for all kinds of events. What's key here, is determining what makes your cupcakes stand out from the rest? That is the question you should answer when developing a marketing/advertising plan. The cupcake business is tough and there are many competitors. You need to find a way to make your cupcake unique so that customers will flock to you.

Making Your Product Unique

First of all, you need to do some research about your competitors. What are they offering? What do their customers like? In business, it's not about selling something that people can buy from other stores. It's about offering something that is **not** found in other shops. What can you put in (or on) your cupcakes to make them different from the other cupcakes? Perhaps, you can add flavors, create custom shapes, and the list goes on. It's up to you. So, spend some time thinking about new ways to improve your cupcakes. Work on creating cupcakes that will make your brand memorable and unique.

Also, consider going into a niche market. For example, earlier I mentioned that if you're nearby a University with a Bumble Bee mascot, you'd want to have Bumble Bee cupcakes. Well that's pretty obvious, right? It's likely that the other 3 nearby cupcake shops already do that too. So now let's think "niche market" here for a minute. What about…. instead of catering to the local sororities and fraternities? Why not choose a certain (large) sorority, then take a box of a dozen free cupcakes decorated with a specific sorority name on it to the front doorstep of the sorority, ring the doorbell, and give it to the board (the sorority's President, VP, Secretary, Treasurer, etc.), along with your business card and personal invitation to come visit the shop? Then the following week, you can do the same with another sorority. So, while these other cupcake shops are sitting there with Bumble Bee cupcakes in their display cases, you've spent a small investment of time and free cupcakes making very powerful and plentiful allies, and your shop will soon be swarming with sorority girls ordering custom-designed cupcakes for every party they throw. Now that's niche marketing. And I hope you understand here, that it goes without saying, this was just one example of many. The concept is to think creatively, and "think niche."

Marketing and Advertising

Now that you have a unique product, you need to tell people about it. Think about marketing strategies that can help you reach your target customers. One of the best ways to market and advertise your product is to have a solid online presence. To do that, you need to have a website for your cupcake business. Having your own website tells people that you are serious about your business. Also, customers can contact you easily through the site and browse your products more conveniently. You can offer product information such as cupcake flavors, designs and prices. People should also be able to order directly through your website.

Another way to promote your business is through the use of social networking sites. A lot of people are on Twitter and Facebook, so you can utilize these to connect with potential clients. Through social networking, you can reach family, friends, colleagues, acquaintances, and let them know about your delicious cupcakes. Make sure to lead them to your website and provide the address of your cupcake store.

Review websites are also key when it comes to this industry. There's no reason on earth why your shop shouldn't be on the Yelp app. If your cupcakes are good, your service is dependable, and your counter staff is friendly, you'll be flooded with good reviews in no time.

Nothing beats word-of-mouth advertisement, though. When your cupcakes are scrumptious and people love them, they'll talk to family and friends. That is still the best kind of advertisement - coming from people that have tried the product and are satisfied with it. So, make sure that your products and service is nothing short of excellent.

New businesses can always benefit from the standard ways of advertising. Newspaper publications as well pamphlets announcing the grand opening of your cupcake shop are tried-and-true ways to catch people's attention.

As time goes by, you need to review your marketing strategies. You should be able to adapt your marketing techniques to the changing times. What might have worked years ago might not be applicable today. Choose the best marketing and advertising strategies for your cupcake business and don't think of the expenses as a loss, rather an investment for the future of your cupcake business. □

Conclusion

Starting a cupcake business is a journey. A really fun, exciting, delicious, and colorful one. It all started from an idea that gradually became a reality as you worked on making it come true. Now that you have come so far, the journey continues.

In every kind of business, the most important aspect is the customers. Without customers, no business will thrive. When you start a cupcake business, you need to know your customers. Exactly who are you targeting, how can you catch their attention, and how can you make them happy? Having a good idea about your customers – and constantly thinking of how you can make your cupcakes appeal to them – can help you create the product they need and offer service that will make them happy.

Creating a customer-focused business has wonderful results. *"Ask not what your cupcake customer can do for you, but what you can do for your cupcake customer."* A lot of companies today fail to put their customers as top priority. The end result is lack of growth, low sales, and eventually bankruptcy. Experienced entrepreneurs understand that customers need to be happy in order to ensure a smooth-running business. In the cupcake business, entrepreneurs need to provide quality cupcakes. But aside from that, customers will always go back to cupcake shops that offer something more. It doesn't have to be a particular flavor or a unique taste. Sometimes, quality service can set one cupcake store apart from the rest.

Learning to value your customers is always a good way to run a business. Satisfied customers will keep on returning and moreover, they will invite other people who are potential customers.

Finally, I'd like to thank you for buying this book! If you enjoyed it or found it helpful, I'd greatly appreciate it if you'd take a moment to leave a review on Amazon. Thank you!

Made in the USA
Monee, IL
11 May 2021